ENTREPRENEUR ACADEMY

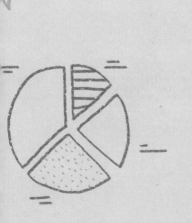

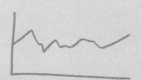

First American Edition 2018
Kane Miller, A Division of EDC Publishing

Copyright © 2018 Quarto Publishing plc

For information contact:
Kane Miller, A Division of EDC Publishing
PO Box 470663
Tulsa, OK 74147-0663
www.kanemiller.com
www.edcpub.com
www.usbornebooksandmore.com

Library of Congress Control Number: 2017958222

Printed in China

ISBN: 978-1-61067-716-5

1 2 3 4 5 6 7 8 9 10

ENTREPRENEUR
ACADEMY

WRITTEN BY
STEVE MARTIN

ILLUSTRATED BY
MAISIE ROBERTSON

Kane Miller
A DIVISION OF EDC PUBLISHING

CONTENTS

Welcome to Entrepreneur Academy 6

CREATIVE SKILLS

New Ideas 8

Better Ideas 10

Design Ideas 12

Right Place, Right Time 14

Testing an Idea 16

Social Entrepreneur 18

Advertising 20

New Trends 22

Branding 24

BUSINESS SKILLS

Costs 26

Selling Price 28

Profit and Loss 30

Balancing Money 32

How to Stand Out 34

Customer Service 36

Making a Pitch 38

Give and Take 40

MANAGEMENT SKILLS

The Manager 42

Finding the Right People 44

Team Building 46

Using Empathy 48

Setting Goals 50

Making a Plan 52

Staying Positive 54

Finding Solutions 56

How to Succeed 58

Get Started 60

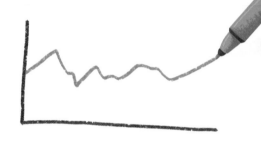

THE MARKETPLACE

Race to the Bank
Game Instructions 64

Stickers

Steps to Success Poster

Race to the Bank Game

WELCOME TO ENTREPRENEUR ACADEMY!

Congratulations. You've now joined Entrepreneur Academy. That's a smart thing to do.

Entrepreneurs are incredibly talented people: they are inventors, designers, employers, managers, bloggers, writers and much more.

They create many of the products and services that we all use. Ask your parents to name all the things you have and use that didn't exist when they were young. It might be a long list and may include things like laptop computers, flat-screen TVs and smartphones.

Entrepreneurs develop new and better products and services. These can improve our lives, create jobs for people and earn money for business owners, their stores, their workers and many others.

As you complete the tasks in this book, you will learn how to:

- think up great ideas
- make a profit
- become a good manager
- create things that people want and need

TRAINEE ENTREPRENEUR

FIRST NAME: Kim

LAST NAME: Peterson

AGE: 26

DATE JOINED: 8.1.2019

yay

Your first task is to fill in the Trainee Entrepreneur card.

As you go through the book, you will study and earn stickers to graduate in Creative Skills, Business Skills and Management Skills.

Best of all, you will have fun learning how to become one of these amazingly creative people!

NEW IDEAS

Entrepreneurs think of new ideas for a business, new things to sell or new ways to help people. Coming up with ideas can seem quite tricky at first. With practice you will find it's easier than you might think!

A good way to find ideas is to **think** about what YOU would like to have. First, think of all the things you do, either for fun or because you have to. Next, think of ways to make these things **better**. For example:

- a way to make **school** more interesting
- a new **theme** for children's parties
- a better way to **store** your toys

- a cool new style of **clothes** or jewelry
- a more **exciting** computer game
- a fun way to **travel** to school

Some of the best ideas help people with **problems** or things they don't like doing. How about a Christmas gift-wrapping business or an emergency room-cleaning service?

NEW THEME PARK

Can you come up with an idea for a new theme park based on your favorite movie? For example, a superhero park where the staff dress in superhero costumes and the rides are named after superheroes who fly, travel superfast or are superstrong!

Write your ideas in the spaces below.

My favorite movie is:

My theme park is called:

Three theme park rides:

Theme park restaurant: (If your movie is *The Wizard of Oz*, you could have "The Yellow Brick Road Diner")

Theme park restaurant dish: (For example, a "SuperBurger")

Three things for sale in the gift shop:

Three staff costumes:

When you have come up with all your theme park ideas, place your Task Complete sticker here.

PLACE STICKER HERE

TASK COMPLETE

BETTER IDEAS

Entrepreneurs don't only come up with brand-new ideas for things to make, do and sell. They also look at what is already being done and think of ways to make it even better.

For example, the **wheel** has been used for thousands of years, but it wasn't until the 19th century that someone came up with the idea of an air-filled tire.

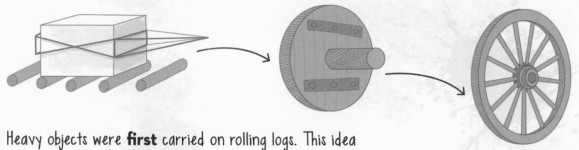

Heavy objects were **first** carried on rolling logs. This idea led to the invention of two wooden wheels joined by an axle.

Later, spokes replaced the solid wood. This **improvement** made wheels lighter and faster.

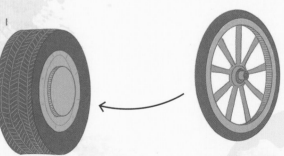

Today, wheels have air-filled rubber **tires** to make rides smoother.

A metal rim was then added to **protect** wheels from damage on bumpy roads.

Entrepreneurs are always thinking of ways to **improve** the world. The next time you come across something that you don't like or find disappointing, try to think how you could make it better.

IMPROVE THREE GREAT EXPERIENCES

How would you make ice cream, bicycling and going to the beach even better? Below are three suggestions for each. Your task is to rank them in order by writing "1" for the best idea, "2" for the second-best idea and "3" for the worst idea.

A. Which flavor would make the best new ice cream?

- ◯ Chocolate banana
- ◯ Meat loaf
- ◯ Salted blueberry

Put 1, 2 or 3 in the circles

B. Which feature could make bicycling safer?

- ◯ An airbag
- ◯ Flashing lights on the saddle
- ◯ Cushioned bicycling clothes

C. Which invention would make going to the beach more fun?

- ◯ A combined camera and face mask for taking pictures under water
- ◯ A beach vacuum cleaner to get all the sand off your feet when you leave
- ◯ A child-size speedboat

TAKE IT FURTHER!
Think of other things that could be improved and bounce ideas around with your friends.

When you have finished ranking the three new ideas, place your Task Complete sticker here.

PLACE STICKER HERE

TASK COMPLETE

DESIGN IDEAS

Entrepreneurs may use design skills to make products from everyday things, such as clothes or jewelry, to create a new "look" that everyone will want.

The clothes we wear—like jeans, skirts, sweaters and shirts—have been around for a long time. By **changing** the shapes, colors and patterns of our clothes, fashion designers create cutting-edge styles that people **want** to buy.

Good design matters for all sorts of other products, too—watches, websites, posters, cars, furniture, phones and food packaging, to name just a few!

T-SHIRT DESIGN

There's nothing more ordinary than a plain T-shirt ... until the designer gets to work! Use markers, crayons or pencils to turn this white T-shirt into one that you would love to wear. Create anything you like—a crazy pattern, or a design based on a TV show, your pet or a favorite sport.

PLACE STICKER HERE

TAKE IT FURTHER!
Transfer your design to a plain T-shirt using fabric pens.

When you have finished your T-shirt Design, place your Task Complete sticker here.

TASK COMPLETE

13

RIGHT PLACE, RIGHT TIME

An entrepreneur can start a business by using an idea that is working well in one place and introducing it somewhere else. First though, the entrepreneur needs to be sure that the idea will be popular in the new area.

A business in one place might not work somewhere else. A store selling **raincoats** may have a lot of customers in a rainy country, but not many in a **sunny** country!

OLD STUFF NEWSPAPER

KING KULLEN was the first supermarket. It opened in New York City in 1930. It was a great idea that **quickly spread** around the world.

KING KULLEN

SANTA CLAUS LAND was the **first** theme park. It opened in 1946, in a town called Santa Claus in Indiana. The entrepreneur who had the idea thought that **visitors** to a town called Santa Claus should be able to visit Santa!

NEW NEIGHBORHOOD BUSINESS

Your task is to decide whether the business ideas below would work in your area. Answering the questions will help you decide.

Put a check in the circle next to the ideas you like and an X next to those you don't think would be so successful.

○ ORANGE ORCHARD
Is the weather warm enough to grow orange trees?

○ INDOOR PLAYGROUND
Are there lots of children in the area?

○ BASKETBALL COACHING
Is basketball popular where you live?

○ SOUVENIR STORE
Do tourists visit your neighborhood?

○ DRY SKI SLOPE
Are there nearby hills for this?

○ DOG-WALKING SERVICE
Are there a lot of dog owners?

○ FOOD DELIVERY
Are grocery stores far away from people's homes?

○ BIKE RENTAL
Are there safe places to ride?

Now think of a business you've seen somewhere else that might catch on in your hometown. It could be a type of store, a leisure activity or a useful service.

MY LOCAL BUSINESS IDEA:

When you have thought of an idea to introduce to your hometown, place your Task Complete sticker here.

PLACE STICKER HERE

TASK COMPLETE

TESTING AN IDEA

Once an entrepreneur has thought of an idea, the next step is to find out whether there are any potential customers.

Here are a few ways to **test** whether an idea will work.

ASK A FOCUS GROUP

An entrepreneur may discuss their idea with a group made up of **people** who might buy or use the product or service. They will ask the group what they like and don't like about it, and how they think the idea could be improved.

CARRY OUT A SALES TEST

If the idea is for a **product** that will be sold in stores, an entrepreneur might make a few samples to sell in one or two stores, to see how popular it is.

DO A SURVEY

A survey is a list of **questions** to find out what people think about a new product or business idea. If carefully designed, a survey can collect useful feedback from a lot of people.

CARRY OUT A SURVEY

Imagine a school principal has given permission to start a school snack service—but it can only sell three snacks. Conduct a survey to help find out the most popular items to sell.

You will need: 5 friends, pen or pencil.

Ask each friend to pick their favorite three snacks from the list. Put "1" next to their most favorite, "2" next to their second favorite and "3" next to their third favorite.

	FRIEND A	FRIEND B	FRIEND C	FRIEND D	FRIEND E
FRUIT					
PIZZA					
CHIPS					
SANDWICH					
PRETZELS					
POPCORN					
COOKIE					
YOGURT					
FRUIT BAR					
JUICE					
HUMMUS AND CARROT STICKS					
CHEESE AND CRACKERS					

Use the results to decide which three items would sell best.

I recommend selling _____,

_____,

and _____.

When you have completed your survey and decided which snacks would sell best, place your Task Complete sticker here.

PLACE STICKER HERE

TASK COMPLETE

SOCIAL ENTREPRENEUR

A social entrepreneur sets up a business to help society—for example, an organization to help house people or to provide better education. The purpose is not usually to make money, but if there is a profit, it is used to improve people's lives in some way.

Some social enterprises are small, **local** businesses, but others are **worldwide** organizations. Look at the examples below.

* **THRIFT STORES** sell donated, secondhand goods in the same way that any store sells things. The profit is used to help people, pay for medical research, or for other causes.

* **HOUSING ORGANIZATIONS** build homes for people to rent cheaply.

* **FAIR-TRADE SCHEMES** make sure that producers get a fair price for their goods. They are often farmers in poorer countries.

* **SOCIAL BANKS** lend money to support businesses and enterprises that help the local community.

* **SOCIAL SUPERMARKETS** sell food cheaply to people who do not have much money to spend.

* **RECYCLING COMPANIES** help the environment by collecting and reusing products.

PLAN A GARAGE SALE

Imagine you are setting up a garage sale, selling unwanted toys, games and books, to raise money for charity. Practice your planning skills by thinking about the order in which you would do the tasks below.

Write "1" in the circle next to the first task, "2" next to the second and so on.

When you have finished, ask a friend to order the tasks too, then compare your answers. Are they the same?

○ Make posters to advertise the sale.

○ Decide on a day and time for your sale.

○ Collect old toys, books and games you no longer want, and ask your friends and family to donate.

○ Ask your neighbors if they would like to participate.

○ Decide how much to sell things for.

○ Decide which charity or good cause you will donate the profits to.

TAKE IT FURTHER!
Now that you've done the planning, why not see if you can hold a real garage sale? Talk to a parent or caregiver.

When you have finished planning your garage sale, place your Task Complete sticker here.

PLACE STICKER HERE

TASK COMPLETE

ADVERTISING

When an entrepreneur launches a new business or product they need to tell everyone about it. One way to do this is by creating eye-catching ads.

Ads attract **customers**, so they need to appeal to the right people. An ad for a new children's comic book must appeal to kids, but an ad for a new garage should be aimed at adults.

ADVERTISING WORDS

Words like these are used in ads to persuade customers to buy a product or service.

NEW	LUXURY	EXCLUSIVE
SENSATIONAL	QUALITY	VALUE
BEST	BUDGET	OFFER

CREATE AN AD

The Giant Super Cheezy is a delicious new type of pizza, made to be shared. Design a colorful ad in the space below to promote it. Draw an eye-catching picture and add a few words chosen from the advertising words panel on page 20.

PLACE STICKER HERE

TAKE IT FURTHER! How would you turn your ad into a TV commercial?

When you have designed and colored your ad, place your Task Complete sticker here.

TASK COMPLETE

NEW TRENDS

The world changes every day and what people want changes, too. A successful entrepreneur needs to keep up with new trends.

TRENDY NEW STUFF.COM

New inventions, products and fashions come and go quickly. Here are some changes that regularly take place.

New stores or restaurants **open** while others close.

There's a craze for **new** toys, games or trading cards.

A new style takes over from the **sneakers** everyone loved last year.

A new **invention** changes the market.

People upgrade their **phone** to the latest model.

TRENDS RESEARCH

Carry out a research project. Fill in the answers to the questions below to show changes in trends where you live.

What new products have your parents bought recently?

Have your parents changed the brand of something they buy?

What is your friend's favorite music, TV program, toy or game?

What clothes or sneakers are popular at the moment?

What digital item do you or your family have (for example, a computer or phone) that you would like to replace with a more up-to-date version?

Have any new leisure businesses, like a restaurant or sports center, opened recently?

Has a business closed down? Why do you think it closed?

PLACE STICKER HERE

When you have finished your Trends Research, place your Task Complete sticker here.

TASK COMPLETE

BRANDING

Entrepreneurs need to make sure that people continue to buy their product. They do this by branding it, so that their product stands out from the crowd and is hard to forget.

Branding includes:

A UNIQUE NAME that everyone will remember.

Yummy Scrummy **Cakes**

THE RIGHT IMAGE—a fun, new airline might be called Bright Skies and have rainbow-patterned planes.

CUTE KITTY SAYS ...
BUY MY PRODUCTS!

MEMORABLE ADS that show characters, slogans or music that instantly connect people to a product.

ENTREPRENEUR INFO

Branding must be **carefully** thought out, so that it appeals to the right market—the customers who will buy the product. For example, **cool** for teenagers, fun and **exciting** for children.

Congratulations! You are now a...

CREATIVE SKILLS
— GRADUATE —

NAME:

The above-named trainee
has now completed the

CREATIVE SKILLS

course.

Entrepreneur Academy would like
to wish you every success
in your career.

GOOD LUCK!

DATE:

COSTS

Some entrepreneurs run businesses that make money by selling things. However, they need to spend money, too. The money a business spends is known as its "costs." Here is a list of the type of costs a store owner may have.

- **ADVERTISING** signs, newspaper and online ads.
- **DELIVERY CHARGES** for stock.
- **EQUIPMENT** such as counters, cash registers and shelves.
- **PRODUCTS** from suppliers.
- **DECOR** such as mirrors, flooring and decoration.
- **UTILITY BILLS** for electricity, fuel, rent and taxes.
- **SALARIES** to pay sales staff.

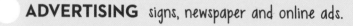

SPOT THE COSTS

In addition to paying suppliers for things to sell, a store also has to spend money on advertising, delivery, salaries and more. Look at the numbered items in the picture. Can you match them to the costs listed on page 26?

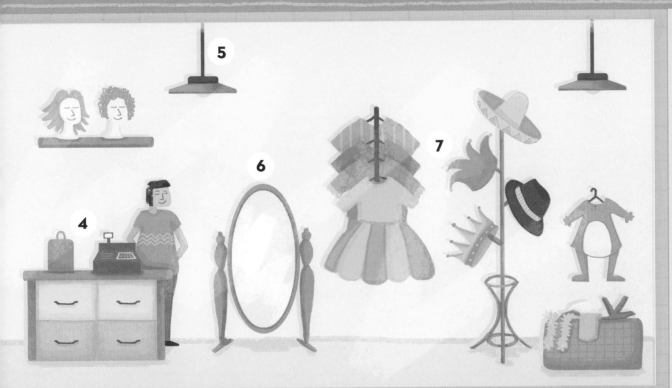

When you have matched the costs to the numbered items in the picture, check your answers below and place your Task Complete sticker here.

PLACE STICKER HERE

Answers: 1. Delivery charges, 2. Salaries, 3. Advertising, 4. Equipment, 5. Utility bills, 6. Decor, 7. Products.

TASK COMPLETE

SELLING PRICE

An entrepreneur needs to know how much to sell things for. If the price is too low, they will lose money. They will also lose money if the price is too high and they don't sell enough products.

Entrepreneurs mostly try to **charge** as much as people are prepared to pay, but lots of things can affect the **price** of products.

PRODUCTION COST

Have you ever wondered why a sports car is more expensive than a normal car? It's because a faster, more luxurious sports car costs more to produce than an everyday car.

$35,000

$150,000

COMPETITION

Knowing what competitors (other businesses) charge is important. For example, if you sell chocolate cookies at $1.00 per package, but another business sells the same cookies for $0.60 per package, you won't sell many cookies!

HIGH DEMAND

The price of popular items always goes up when there are fewer of them. For example, the cost of plane tickets to a favorite vacation destination can rise as more people buy seats and flights fill up.

TICKET

PRICING PRACTICE

Imagine you are running the bakery below. Your task is to fill in the prices on the cards. There are no right or wrong answers—how much you charge will depend on how much you think your customers will pay.

THINGS TO CONSIDER
Ask yourself these questions before you decide on the prices.

- **SIZE** How much is the customer getting for their money?

- **QUALITY** Is this product made from luxury ingredients?

- **APPEARANCE** Does the decoration add something extra?

- **VALUE** Are you offering the customer a good deal?

- **RARITY** Is it a one-off product in high demand?

When you have decided how much to charge and filled in the prices, place your Task Complete sticker here.

PLACE STICKER HERE

TASK COMPLETE

BUSINESS
SKILLS

PROFIT AND LOSS

Entrepreneurs must spend money on their costs and make money on their sales. To be successful, they must make more money than they spend. The money gained is called the profit.

MAKING A PROFIT

If you spend **$5** on 5 toys then sell them for **$2** each, you will make a profit.

$5   BUY → $1 $1 $1 $1 $1   SELL → $2 $2 $2 $2 $2   = $10 SALES   − $5 COSTS   = $5 PROFIT

MAKING A LOSS

If you spend **$5** to buy 5 toys then sell them for **40 cents** each, you will make a loss.

$5   BUY → $1 $1 $1 $1 $1   SELL → $0.40 $0.40 $0.40 $0.40 $0.40   = $2 SALES   − $5 COSTS   = $3 LOSS

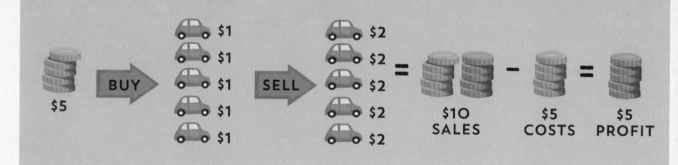

PROFIT AND LOSS MATH

Are these two businesses making a profit or a loss? First, figure out the total costs and total sales figures. Next, subtract the total costs from the total sales. Write the answers in the spaces and then circle either Profit or Loss.

BUSINESS: ICE CREAM PARLOR

COSTS		SALES	
Supplies	$200	Ice cream	$400
Rent	$100	Soft drinks	$200
Bills	$100	TOTAL SALES	
Salaries	$100		
TOTAL COSTS			

TOTAL SALES - TOTAL COSTS = _____ PROFIT / LOSS

Add the figures in the columns to get the totals.

BUSINESS: BIKE DELIVERIES

COSTS		SALES	
Bikes	$500	Express deliveries	$600
Bills	$200	Normal deliveries	$300
Salaries	$300	TOTAL SALES	
TOTAL COSTS			

TOTAL SALES - TOTAL COSTS = _____ PROFIT / LOSS

Subtract the total costs from the total sales and circle Profit or Loss.

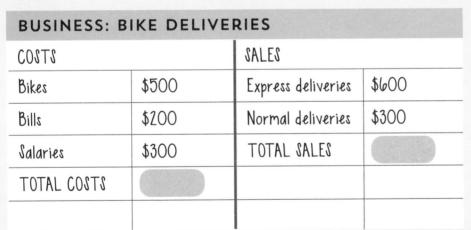

PLACE STICKER HERE

When you have worked out the Profit and Loss Math for each business, check your answers below and place your Task Complete sticker here.

Answers: Ice cream parlor makes a $100 profit. Bike deliveries makes a $100 loss.

TASK COMPLETE

BALANCING MONEY

Every day, a business spends money and makes money. It is very important to keep track of the money that goes out (expenses) and the money that comes in (income), so that the business stays healthy.

Study this example of a swim club's accounts. Notice how the **balance** goes **down** when money is paid out and goes **up** when money comes in.

STARTING BALANCE
This shows how much money you have to begin with.

DATE	DESCRIPTION	MONEY IN	MONEY OUT	BALANCE
May 1	Starting balance	$0	$0	**$500**
May 2	Pool rental	$0	$100	$400
May 3	Swimmers' fees	$300	$0	$700
May 4	Staff salaries	$0	$100	$600
May 5	Swimsuit sale	$50	$0	**$650**

FINAL BALANCE
That's $150 more than the starting balance.

Besides telling you how much you are making, keeping track of expenses and income is useful—it can show you where you might save money or how to make more of it.

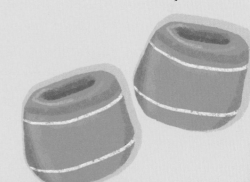

COMPLETE THE ACCOUNTS

Your task is to calculate the daily balances for a dog-walking business. Make sure you work across each row from left to right, adding the Money In amount or subtracting the Money Out amount from the previous day's balance.

DAY	DESCRIPTION	MONEY IN	MONEY OUT	BALANCE
Monday	Starting balance	$0	$0	$800
Tuesday	Van repair	$0	$200	
Wednesday	Customer fees	$600	$0	
Thursday	Staff salaries	$0	$500	
Friday	Puppy-training class	$200	$0	
Saturday	Advertising	$0	$100	

Can you think of another useful service the dog-walking business could offer to make extra money? Write down your idea here:

_____

_____

_____

_____

Write the daily balance in the blank spaces.

When you have filled in the daily balances, check your answers below and then place your Task Complete sticker here.

PLACE STICKER HERE

Answers: Tuesday: $600, Wednesday: $1,200, Thursday: $700, Friday: $900, Saturday: $800.

TASK COMPLETE

33

HOW TO STAND OUT

If only one company in the world made cars, it would make huge profits. Not only would everyone have to buy their cars from it, but the company could charge any price it liked.

Luckily, this doesn't happen. Real businesses **compete** with each other to attract customers. They try to offer **good-quality** products and services at competitive prices.

Look at these two **lemonade stands**. It's not difficult to see which one will attract more customers.

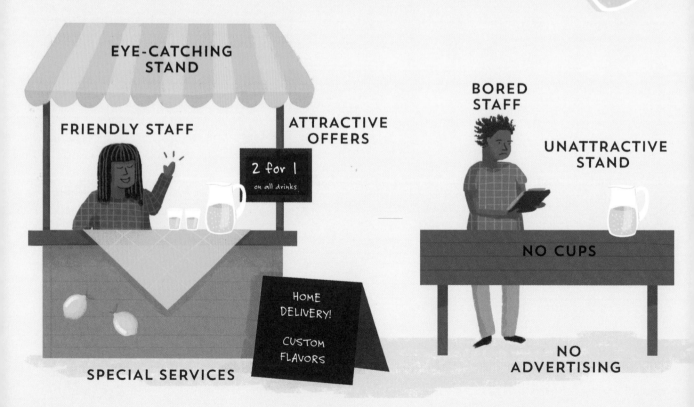

EYE-CATCHING STAND

FRIENDLY STAFF

ATTRACTIVE OFFERS

2 for 1
on all drinks

HOME DELIVERY!

CUSTOM FLAVORS

SPECIAL SERVICES

BORED STAFF

UNATTRACTIVE STAND

NO CUPS

NO ADVERTISING

WINDOW DISPLAY

Many stores attract customers with eye-catching window displays that help them stand out from the competition. Design an exciting window display for your new candy store.

Write your store name here.

Write a message to your customers here.

Create a yummy window display to attract customers.

You could draw lots of colorful candy jars or even create a scene made of candy.

When you have drawn and colored your Window Display, place your Task Complete sticker here.

PLACE STICKER HERE

TASK COMPLETE

CUSTOMER SERVICE

A business can't exist without customers. Entrepreneurs need to value their customers and treat them with respect—even when things go wrong!

Taking care of **customers** is an important skill. Study these Do's and Don't's.

DO
- Smile
- Be polite
- Listen
- Solve problems

DON'T
- Be grumpy
- Be rude
- Ignore
- Refuse to help

ROLE PLAY

There may be times when a customer is angry, confused or upset. Practice your customer-service skills by working with a friend on the role play below.

Decide who will be the customer and who will play the entrepreneur. Read the role-play descriptions carefully before acting out the situation.

CUSTOMER'S ROLE

* You are upset after a horrible day at the theme park.

* Half the rides were closed, and there were long lines for the rest.

* Most of the rides were too scary for your little brother, who is only six.

ENTREPRENEUR'S ROLE

* Listen to the customer's complaint without interrupting.

* Apologize and tell them that some rides were closed for safety reasons due to bad weather.

* Explain that closing some rides caused long lines at the other rides.

* Politely point out that the rides are clearly advertised for ages 10 years and older. Offer a free ticket to a nearby theme park for younger children.

When you and your friend have finished the customer-service role play, place your Task Complete sticker here.

PLACE STICKER HERE

TASK COMPLETE

MAKING A
—PITCH—

An entrepreneur who comes up with a new service or product may need the support of a larger business to help them launch their idea. To do this, they need to know how to deliver a business pitch. A pitch is when you present your idea for a service or product, and explain the good things about it. An entrepreneur may only have a **few minutes** to talk about their product. To make sure their pitch stands out, many entrepreneurs follow the **four Ps**.

PREPARE

Plan what you are going to say and do.

PRACTICE

Rehearse your pitch in advance.

PROPS

Write key words on **flash cards**, make a poster or take a sample of your product.

PRESENTATION

Dress nicely, smile, make eye contact and be **confident**.

PLAN A PITCH

In the space below, plan a fast-paced pitch that will convince your audience to try something that you love. Choose to pitch your favorite book, movie, food, game or toy.

1. Decide on your product and write its name here.

2. Write three key words that describe it.
   1.
   2.
   3.

3. Give two reasons why it is better than the competition.
   1.
   2.

4. Decide on three props that will help your pitch.
   1.
   2.
   3.

Now, find an empty room and practice delivering your pitch out loud!

TAKE IT FURTHER! Time to pitch for real! Why not present your favorite product to your friends, family or class?

When you have finished planning your pitch, place your Task Complete sticker here.

PLACE STICKER HERE

TASK COMPLETE

GIVE AND —TAKE—

To get the price they want for their product or service, an entrepreneur must be good at negotiation—talking to people and reaching an agreement that makes everybody happy.

You may not realize it, but you **negotiate** with other people all the time. Here are some examples.

You want to watch **TV**, but your friend wants to play soccer. Instead of having an argument, you find a way to **agree**.

You want to **borrow** your sister's bike, and you want to make sure she will lend it to you. So you **offer** to trade something or do her a favor, such as cleaning her room.

**ENTREPRENEUR
INFO**

Congratulations! You are now a...

BUSINESS SKILLS
—GRADUATE—

NAME:

The above-named trainee
has now completed the

BUSINESS SKILLS

course.

Entrepreneur Academy would like
to wish you every success
in your career.

GOOD LUCK!

DATE:

THE MANAGER

Entrepreneurs need to be able to organize—or manage—people and activities, so that their business runs smoothly.

A manager's job is to:

check on progress

decide if things can be done better

make sure the people, materials and time to do each activity are in place

communicate clearly so that everyone knows what to do

identify what work needs to be done

build a team of people

break the work down into small tasks

deal with problems

support their team

42

IDENTIFY YOUR MANAGEMENT SKILLS

Would it surprise you to learn that you are already using management skills? Read the four skills below and see if you can recognize times when you have used them. Look at the ideas to help you, then write your answers in the spaces.

Skill 1: Identifying what work needs to be done

I have done this when...

_____
_____
_____
_____
_____

Skill 2: Breaking down the work into small tasks

I have done this when...

_____
_____
_____
_____

IDEAS
* Cleaning my room
* Planning a party
* Doing homework

Skill 3: Communicating clearly so that everyone knows what to do

I have done this when...

_____
_____
_____
_____

IDEAS
* Playing a game
* A class group activity
* Deciding what to have for dinner

Skill 4: Supporting a team

I have done this when...

_____
_____
_____
_____
_____

PLACE STICKER HERE

When you have identified the times when you have used management skills, place your Task Complete sticker here.

TASK COMPLETE

FINDING THE RIGHT PEOPLE

A manager needs to have the right people on their team. They will carry out an interview with each person who wants to join. An interview is a meeting to find out if they are the best person for a job.

To get the information they need, a manager must ask the right interview questions, like these:

WILL THE PERSON FIT IN?

* What can you tell me about **yourself**?
* What do you **do** in your free time?
* Why should I **hire** you?

WHY DO THEY WANT THE JOB?

* Why did you **apply** for this job?
* Why do you want to work for this **company**?
* What do you think you will **like** about the job?

WHAT ARE THEIR SKILLS?

* What are your **strengths**?
* What **qualifications** do you have?
* Have you taken any **training** courses?

WHAT IS THEIR WORK EXPERIENCE?

* Can you tell me about the **jobs** you have had?
* Why do you want to **leave** the job you have now?
* What **successes** have you had in your work?

44

JOB INTERVIEW

Practice your interview skills on a friend. First, ask what their dream job would be. Next, choose one question to ask them from three of the four categories on page 44. Fill in your friend's name and dream job, and write down your interview questions in the spaces below.

NAME:

DREAM JOB:

INTERVIEW QUESTION 1:

INTERVIEW QUESTION 2:

INTERVIEW QUESTION 3:

Now carry out the interview. Make sure you smile and are friendly and encouraging! People talk more when they are relaxed, and you will learn more about a person by listening to what they have to say.

When you have filled in the form and carried out the Job Interview, place your Task Complete sticker here.

PLACE STICKER HERE

TASK COMPLETE

TEAM BUILDING

People achieve more when they work well together, so once a manager has found the right people, they need to mold them into a winning team.

These mountaineers must use the same teamwork to reach the summit that a good manager **builds** into their team.

"Hold the rope while I climb up."

"Keep going, Sophie! You're doing great."

TRUST Team members trust each other and know everyone will do their job.

FRIENDSHIP People work better with people they get along with.

"Jack, you're strong. Hold the rope for the others."

"It's getting dark. What should we do?"

DIVIDING WORK The team decides who is best at each part of a task.

"Emma's hurt. Let's help her together."

COMMUNICATION Everyone needs to know about the challenges and discuss them.

SHARING WORK When someone needs help, the rest of the team supports them.

TEAMWORK CHALLENGE

Find two friends and practice your team-building skills with this fun challenge. All you have to do is carry a balloon from a starting point to a bucket. But you are not allowed to touch it with your hands, arms or feet while you move it!

You will need: large indoor or outdoor space, a bucket, a marker (such as a sweater), a balloon, two friends.

1. Place the marker on the ground as the starting line. Place the bucket about 12 feet away.

2. Decide who will be Player 1. They are allowed to touch the balloon with their hands, but must stay at the starting line.

3. Discuss how Players 2 and 3 can carry the balloon between them. With Player 1's help, position the balloon as securely as you can.

4. Carefully carry the balloon without letting it fall, and drop it into the bucket.

Carry out this challenge three times, so that all three players have a turn being Player 1.

PLACE STICKER HERE

When you have had three attempts at the Teamwork Challenge, place your Task Complete sticker here.

TASK COMPLETE

USING EMPATHY

The best managers support their team. If someone is upset, worried or making mistakes in their work, a manager can use a skill called empathy to try to help them. Empathy means being able to understand other people's feelings.

Here are **six steps** to help learn how someone else is feeling.

1. **LISTEN:** give people time to talk.

2. **IMAGINE** how you would feel in their situation.

3. **SHOW** the person that you care.

4. **THINK:** when did something similar happen to you?

5. **ENQUIRE:** ask how the person feels.

6. **NOTICE:** does the person look sad, frightened or confused?

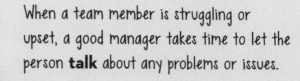

When a team member is struggling or upset, a good manager takes time to let the person **talk** about any problems or issues.

IDENTIFY THE EMPATHY STEPS

In the four situations below, the manager is using empathy to understand how each person is feeling. Can you identify the steps they are using? Write your answers in the spaces—the first one has been done for you.

"You look angry, Kate."

1 Notice

"Don't worry, Lucy. I've done the same thing lots of times."

2

"How are you feeling, Megan?"

3

"I can imagine how busy and stressed you must be."

4

TAKE IT FURTHER!
Next time a friend is angry or upset, use your empathy skills to help them feel better.

When you have identified the four empathy steps being used, check your answers at the bottom of the page and place your Task Complete sticker here.

PLACE STICKER HERE

Answers: 1. Notice, 2. Think, 3. Enquire, 4. Imagine.

TASK COMPLETE

SETTING GOALS

Before starting their new business, an entrepreneur needs to set a clear goal for the business, and smaller goals for everyone working on their team.

For example, the **business goal** for a new restaurant might be:

SELL THE BEST MEALS IN TOWN TO 100 CUSTOMERS A DAY

So, the **smaller goals** for the team members might be:

CHEF: cook fresh, tasty food every day.

WAITER: provide friendly, helpful service so that people come back.

MANAGER: think of new ways to attract customers.

Setting clear goals like these makes it easy to check on **progress** toward them and make **changes** if things aren't going well.

ACTIONS MATCH

To help the restaurant team succeed, their goals are broken into sets of separate actions. Your task is to match each team member to the correct set of actions.

MANAGER

WAITER

CHEF

Actions set A

* Be polite and smile.

* Don't keep customers waiting.

* Clear away dirty plates quickly.

Team member:

Write your answer here.

Actions set B

* Use only fresh ingredients and vary the menu.

* Make sure the food is well cooked and looks inviting.

* Check that the work areas are clean and that food is stored safely.

Team member:

Actions set C

* Offer special-price deals and a children's menu.

* Get feedback from customers about their experience.

* Make sure there are enough supplies.

Team member:

PLACE STICKER HERE

When you have matched the restaurant team members to their actions, check your answers below and then put your Task Complete sticker here.

TASK COMPLETE

MAKING A PLAN

Entrepreneurs make a plan to help their business succeed. A plan contains the steps they must take to reach a goal. It helps them to work in an organized way, without forgetting anything.

We use plans to achieve goals all the time in everyday life. Look at this **mind-map** plan for a well-run school day:

* Children are picked up promptly.

* Teachers take turns to supervise after-school activities.

* Classes start and end on time.

* Teachers and children know which classes they will have.

AFTER SCHOOL

SCHEDULE

WELL-ORGANIZED SCHOOL DAY

LUNCH BREAK

LESSONS

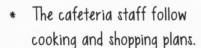

* The cafeteria staff follow cooking and shopping plans.

* Food is ready to serve on time.

* Lesson plans are worked out in advance.

* Teachers follow the right lesson plans.

MAKE A MIND MAP

Your goal is to organize your next birthday party. Fill in the blank spaces on the mind-map plan and see where your planning takes you. Try not to leave anything out and use extra paper if your map grows bigger than the page!

TIME AND PLACE

GUESTS

MY BIRTHDAY PARTY

FOOD AND DRINKS

THEME

When you have finished making your birthday party mind map, place your Task Complete sticker here.

PLACE STICKER HERE

TASK COMPLETE

STAYING POSITIVE

Entrepreneurs need to have a positive, can-do attitude. Being positive spreads—if you're upbeat and confident, your team will be too! They will work harder and enjoy what they do. They won't be put off by problems that come up, either.

Here are some **ideas** of how you can be a positive manager.

* Listen to your team and be **interested** in their ideas.

* Say "thank you"—just because people work for you doesn't mean that you can take their **support** for granted.

* Reward good work with **a smile** and a "well done!"

* **Have fun** and make sure your team does too. People perform better when they **enjoy** coming to work.

This doesn't mean that you can ignore **problems**—in fact, it means the opposite! Instead of feeling angry or upset if things **go wrong**, a positive manager works quickly to **fix** a problem, so that it won't happen again.

PRACTICE BEING POSITIVE

The more you practice being positive, the more it will come naturally. Starting today, use this chart to write down the best thing that happens to you every day for a week, and how it made you feel.

DAY	THE BEST THING	HOW THIS MADE ME FEEL
Monday	I saw a double rainbow!	Lucky

At the end of the week, you'll see that good things happen all the time, even on bad days, so it makes sense to be enthusiastic and cheerful!

When you have finished filling in the positive practice chart, place your Task Complete sticker here.

PLACE STICKER HERE

TASK COMPLETE

MANAGEMENT
SKILLS

FINDING SOLUTIONS

An entrepreneur has to be ready to deal with anything that may affect their business. Look at these typical problems and the solutions for fixing them.

SOLUTION: Use the time to catch up with cleaning, paperwork or changing the stock display.

SOLUTION: Always keep some emergency supplies in your storeroom.

SOLUTION: Call another team member who has the day off to ask if they can come to work. Offer them extra pay if they can.

PROBLEM: It's raining heavily so there aren't any customers.

PROBLEM: The delivery truck has broken down, leaving the business without any products to sell.

PROBLEM: A member of the team is sick and cannot come to work.

SOLVE THE PROBLEMS

Can you find the solutions for these two problems? One is trickier than the other!

1. A new gym has put on exciting activity sessions for children ages 9 to 12. These take place on Wednesdays from 10:00 a.m. until 12:00 p.m. But, after three weeks, not a single child has turned up! What do you think the problem might be and how could it be solved?

The problem is: _____

_____

The solution could be: _____

_____

200 lb.   200 lb.

2. Two workers are arguing over which of them will move 200 pounds of rocks and which will move 200 pounds of sand. The first says it is unfair to have to move 200 pounds of heavy rocks because these weigh much more than 200 pounds of light sand.

The solution could be: _____

_____

_____

_____

When you have written down solutions to the problems, check the answers below and place your Task Complete sticker here.

Answers: 1. All the children are at school at this time. Solution: The sessions should be after school or on weekends. 2. Explain that 200 lb. of rocks weigh the same as 200 lb. of sand.

HOW TO SUCCEED

When an entrepreneur has created a business, they don't relax. Instead, they think of ways to keep improving their business, or they might set up a brand-new enterprise.

They do this by:

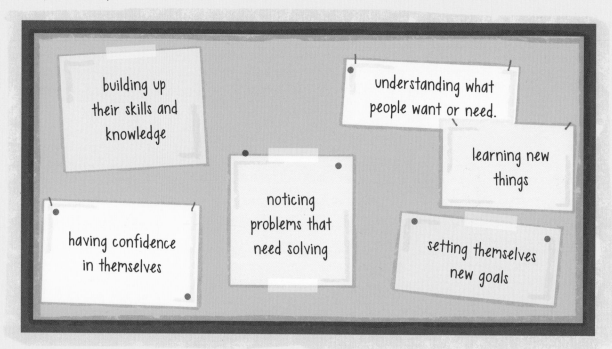

building up their skills and knowledge

understanding what people want or need.

learning new things

having confidence in themselves

noticing problems that need solving

setting themselves new goals

GIVING BACK

The most **successful** entrepreneurs can make a lot of money! Instead of keeping it all for themselves, many like to give a share to charities, or use it to help **a cause** they strongly believe in. They may encourage the people who work for them to give back, too—by taking part in **community projects**, sponsored events to raise money, or by taking time off work to volunteer with a charity.

SOME FAMOUS ENTREPRENEURS STARTED IN A SMALL WAY.

When **THOMAS EDISON** was a child he sold candy and newspapers on trains. He grew up to become the **inventor** of the light bulb, record player and movie camera.

WALT DISNEY grew up on a farm and loved drawing animals. He set up a cartoon studio and created **Mickey Mouse**, the first Disney character, in 1928. Disney movies and theme parks are world famous today.

MADAM C. J. WALKER noticed the need for hair and beauty products for black women, so she made her own using **homemade** recipes. Her products were so popular that she set up both a business and a hair-care training school.

The cofounder of Apple, **STEVE JOBS**, was **often bored** at school but loved electronics. He started his famous **computer** company in the family garage when he was 21.

J. K. ROWLING, the author, screenwriter and creator, wrote the first **Harry Potter** book in her spare time. Eleven publishers rejected her idea before the **twelfth** said yes!

ENTREPRENEUR INFO

GET STARTED

Now you can put your training into practice. Here are some ideas for home, school or neighborhood enterprises to raise money for causes or charities. You can go it alone or set up a business with a friend. Make sure you recruit an adult helper for your team!

SERVICES
Find out if there's a need in your neighborhood for:

* Dog walking
* Pet feeding
* Car washing
* Gift wrapping
* Face painting

MAKE AND SELL
Create these fun products to sell.

* Bath bombs
* Cookies and cakes
* Greeting cards
* Cool bracelets

SOW AND SELL
Grow a profit from small seed packets.

* Vegetables
* Flowers
* Herbs

SHOW TIME

Put on a show! Design the tickets and a poster.

* Magic tricks
* Talent show
* Pet show
* A play
* Art exhibition

COLLECT AND SELL

Hold a garage sale. Ask family and friends for unwanted:

* Clothes and shoes
* Toys, books and games

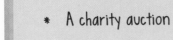

FUNDRAISER

Organize a school or community fundraising event.

* A charity auction
* Dress-up day
* Sports day
* Coloring wall

MORE IDEAS

Ask an adult to help you check out books and websites for more great ideas.
Write some here:

Congratulations! You are now a...

MANAGEMENT SKILLS
— GRADUATE —

NAME:

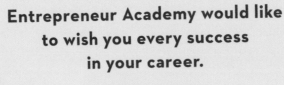

The above-named trainee
has now completed the

MANAGEMENT SKILLS

course.

Entrepreneur Academy would like
to wish you every success
in your career.

GOOD LUCK!

DATE:

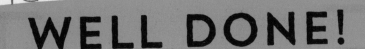

WELL DONE!

You have successfully completed all your tasks
and finished your trainee entrepreneur's course.

You are now ready to graduate from Entrepreneur Academy.

**AS PART OF YOUR GRADUATION CEREMONY, YOU SHOULD READ
THE ENTREPRENEUR'S CODE BELOW AND PROMISE TO FOLLOW IT.**

Once you have done this, you can collect your final qualification.

1. I will be a creative thinker and will remain alert to new ideas.

2. I will notice needs and solve problems that will make
   people's lives better.

3. I will work hard to create products and services that
   people want to buy.

4. I will support and encourage the team working for me.

5. I will respect my customers at all times.

6. I understand the importance of giving back
   and helping others.

7. I will support new entrepreneurs
   in their work and in keeping
   the Entrepreneur's Code.

Draw or glue a
photo of your
face here.

SIGNED:

- - - - - - - - - - - - - - - -

THE MARKETPLACE

- Steps to Success Poster
- Race to the Bank Game
- Press-out Price Tags
  (on the flaps of the cover)
- Stickers

RACE TO THE BANK GAME INSTRUCTIONS

This is a game for 2 people.

You have started a new business, costing $1,000 to set up. Your goal is to make at least $20,000, faster than the other player. You need to keep a tally of the amount of money you have as you play. (Start your tally with –$1,000. You will need to earn that back first.) Take turns to roll the dice and move around the board. Whenever you land on a money rectangle, collect the amount shown on the rectangle. If you land on a Chance Card rectangle, you must pick a card and follow the instructions to gain or lose money. Once you have collected $20,000 or more, you can "Race to the Bank." The first player to arrive at the bank is the winner.